VIKING
YOUTUBE MARKETING

Viking YouTube Marketing Page

Chapter 1:

Introduction

Established in 2005, YouTube is one of the first global social networks around, and its relevance continues to do nothing but grow. The video content posted, viewed, and shared on YouTube can be watched on desktops, laptops, notebooks and smartphones—any time of day or night. YouTube attracts a larger range of demographics across all ages, hobbies, interests, and careers than any other social media platform— and YouTube videos can generate high search engine page rank. If that's not enough, the combined audio/visual makes content more memorable than plain written text.

The Numbers Speak for Themselves

As the demand for quality video content increases, YouTube continues gain more subscribers. Below is a closer look at some of the benefits to creating an organic video marketing strategy.

Worldwide, YouTube has over 1 billion users (yes, a billion) and a whopping 30 million of them watch videos every day. An astounding 5 billion videos are viewed each day, totaling in over 500 million hours of daily viewing. Over 300,000 new videos are uploaded daily. 80% of people ages 18 to 49 regularly watch YouTube videos. Over 50% of YouTube videos are viewed on mobile devices. The average mobile viewing session lasts 40 minutes, so there's an amazing opportunity to connect with your audience there. 38% of users are female and 62% are male.

So clearly the general stats and demographics are there and by themselves they warrant using YouTube as a marketing channel, but the marketing-related stats are even more compelling.

Today, around 87% of online marketers use video content. One-third of online activity is watching videos. 92% of mobile video viewers share the content they watch. When given the choice, 59% of executives will choose video content over written articles. Video drives a 157% increase in organic traffic from SERPs. The click thru rate of emails with videos is 96% higher. Content retention increases from 10% to 95% when comparing video to text. Users spend 88% longer on websites with video. Blog posts with video attract 3x more inbound links. Adding video to ads increases engagement by 22%. And 85% of businesses have in-house staff who curate video content, which shows you how important all your competitors think video marketing is.

That settles it. You obviously need to be marketing on YouTube. Next up, we'll talk about establishing YouTube marketing goals.

Chapter 2:

YouTube Marketing Goals

Establishing marketing goals is critical to the success of your YouTube marketing. Countless entrepreneurs and businesses have setup an YouTube presence, made a few posts, and then let it sit untouched for months or even years. This is usually due to a lack or absence of goals. So, before you even begin establishing any sort of YouTube presence or strategy, you need to establish clear marketing goals.

Your goals should be specific, measurable, and attainable. They can be long term, short term, or a mix of both. Deadlines and milestones can be helpful as well. "I want to increase my social following" would be an example of a bad goal that will likely result in your marketing efforts petering out after a while because there are no specific milestones. "I want to gain 1,000 likes by Christmas" is an example of a good goal. It's specific, measurable, and certainly attainable. Below are some examples of the various goal categories you might be interested in.

Traffic to Website (Sales, Leads, Content)

Probably one of the most popular goals of YouTube Marketing is to funnel your YouTube traffic back to your own web properties. After all, most businesses don't do business "on" YouTube . You're leveraging YouTube to obtain traffic and convert that YouTube traffic into brand-followers, leads, prospects, and customers. So maybe your goal is to get people to a landing page with a free offer where they can subscribe to your list and become a lead. Maybe they're being sent to a sales page or an eCommerce store. Maybe you just want to do some content marketing and send them to your blog. Whatever the case, the end goal for a lot of businesses will likely be bringing YouTube traffic AWAY from YouTube and over to their own web properties.

Social Following (aka YouTube as Autoresponder)

In this goal category, your aim is to build a large number of followers. The reason we also refer to this as "YouTube as Autoresponder" is because the main sought-after benefit here is to increase the number of people who will see your uploads in their feeds. In this sense, your YouTube posts become similar to sending out email broadcasts via your autoresponder. If you grow a large enough community, this can be very beneficial and if your content is engaging enough to get a lot of traction in the form of likes, comments, subscribes and shares, you can significantly increase the range of your organic reach into people's feeds.

Passive Presence

Some businesses might have purely passive goals. Simply being present and discoverable inside YouTube is a benefit that has wider appeal and greater utility than you may think. In many cases, a company's YouTube presence might supersede or at least augment what was once the role of a blog, assuming most of your content can be conveyed in the form of or attached to videos. When people come across this content of yours and look at your account they can see some basic info about your brand or business and you can get some traffic to your website. This same approach can also be used for events, communities, and brands.

Brand Awareness

Another goal that's less thought about might be spreading brand awareness and recognition. If you're just starting out, there's a good chance your brand might be in need of a jumpstart. If nobody's ever heard of you, a great way to increase recognition is to simply create and share unique, helpful, or entertaining content and get your name, logo, and overall brand identity in front of as many people as possible as many times as possible. If this is your goal, you want to avoid being salesy in the beginning. Ensure you're focused almost entirely on posting helpful, relevant, or entertaining content.

Expand Existing Audiences

If you've already got an audience, your goal might be to make it bigger. This can be done via several social marketing methods. Sharing viral content, either curated or created yourself, can lead to a huge increase in your YouTube audience. Although creating your own viral content like that can be great, if you don't have the time or means to do so, you can simply leverage existing content that's already proven itself to be viral by curating/re-sharing it with your own comments or angle added to it. Obviously, you don't want to actually steal and re-upload someone else's videos. We're talking doing a little video review or commentary about a content piece. Also, a few humorous videos can't hurt either. Other ways to expand existing audiences can include contests, sweepstakes, and gamification. Assuming your offers/prizes are compelling enough, incentivized sharing, liking, and subscribing can be very effective. Just ensure your methods are permitted by YouTube's Terms of Service.

Enhancing or Repairing Public Relations

Do you want to set your company apart in the public eye? Do you want to associate your brand with feelings of good will and community involvement? Was your business recently involved in a controversial incident that requires damage control?

It doesn't take a humiliating public catastrophe to make PR enhancement a good idea. This is a goal that any business can engage in. Non-sales related campaigns can include videos that foster positive values and goodwill or even involvement in social movements (be careful not alienate half your prospects) and noble causes. Did your business recently donate to a charity, build a school in a third world country, serve food at a local pantry? These are all things to post about. These don't necessarily need to be about things that your business participated in. They can be content about general things like a heart-warming video about helping the poor or caring for the elderly. Special holidays like Christmas,

Thanksgiving, or Mother's Day also present opportunities to leverage emotions, foster goodwill, and enhance your PR.

Market Research

A hugely beneficial goal of YouTube marketing is market research. If you're just starting your business or going down a new path, YouTube can be an excellent place to learn more about your audience and your market. This can be done in a structured way with things like mentioning surveys and questionnaires at the end of videos and linking to them in the description, or in a less structured way by simply engaging with your audience, commenting, asking questions, and so on. Also, lurking or conversing in YouTube channels or the comments of videos related to your industry can teach you a ton about what your customers want and who they are. Beyond that, you can monitor your competitors' accounts and posts to see what their customers like and what they're complaining about so you can adjust your business accordingly. Creating your own account, posting, and engaging within it is another great way to get a constant stream of market/audience data flowing into your business. Ultimately, your goal should be to come up with one or two ideal customer avatars that you can then base your marketing and product development on.

All of the goals you've learned about in this section require some sort of presence on YouTube. Getting that presence started is what we're going to talk about next.

Chapter 3:

Getting Started On YouTube

The first step in getting started on YouTube is to create your company Channel. If you already have a company Channel, you can organically optimize your Channel with the tips below.

Selecting Your Channel Name

In a perfect world, your Channel name will be your business name. If your business name is already taken, get as close to your business name as possible. For example, you could abbreviate your name or add or delete identifiers such as "Inc."

If the product or service you are promoting is singular, or in a clear niche—try looking for a creative, catching, and memorable Channel name. However, you must be forward thinking when selecting your Channel name. For example, what if you expand your product line? Would you have 2 separate Channels, or one cohesive Channel?

If appropriate, you could even use your first and last name as your Channel name. Consider keywords, but remember that keywords are in constant flux.

Currently, you can create up to 50 Channels. But in most cases, it is more strategic (and time-efficient) to have one Channel with lots of videos and playlists than several singular Channels. But we will talk more about strategy in the next chapter.

Optimizing Your Images

If you are familiar with optimizing blog post and website images *prior* to uploading them to your website, the concept is the same. This is one of those tiny details that many people underestimate, or simply don't know exists—but which can go a long way in organic YouTube and search engine optimization.

The best way to optimize your images is to use Google Trends or a paid keyword tool to identify the best keywords. Then, name and save your YouTube profile pic and banner with the most suitable keywords. Even if you are using your company logo, you must first name and save it with your relevant keywords.

Even if you maintain the same profile pick and banner, update them both with new keywords on a quarterly basis.

Don't Just Copy And Paste Your About Section

It is tempting to simply copy and paste the About section of your website in YouTube and your other online platforms, sales sites, and social media Channels. However, it is important to write unique descriptions for each of your online descriptions. This minimizes the amount of duplicate online content, but it also ensures you take the time to write a unique description relevant to the purpose of each online profile. For example, your YouTube description should touch on the value you plan to add with your Channel.

Once you have written a few unique sentences or paragraphs, take the time to add the About section links to your website, other social platforms, and top trending news.

Chapter 4:

Content & Optimization Strategy

Before you begin creating your video content, you want to develop a video content strategy. Avoid the common temptation to just post about your products and services, and consider how you can create relevant video playlists which will meet a wide range of your target audience's needs. Yes, this can include sales—but it's time to think outside the box. Posting just a handful of relevant and high-quality videos is always better than posting a high volume of useless videos. Use any combination of the ideas below as inspiration as content your customers will engage with.

Start with your FAQs

An excellent place to begin is to take a look at your customers most frequently asked questions. This can include industry questions and product questions alike. Answer the questions via a video or video series, and drive instant engagement.

Educational or Instructional

Educational and instructional "How To" videos are another popular choice. Here are a few examples:

- Does your product require assembly? Great create a step-by-step video of how to put it together.
- Do you sell a digital product? Create a video of the screen shots for performing common (or advanced) functions using your software or app.
- Do you sell a tool that can be used for a versatile range of functions? Create a video highlighting its most common features. For example, a makeup demo.
- Is there an adjacent software, product, or tool your customers use? Create a video on how to integrate with your product.

You can even create videos that you can use to train your team—and post them online in an invitation-only video playlist.

Client Testimonials

Your passionate and happy customers are often eager to share their great experience with others. The next time you receive a raving online review or direct email, ask the customer if they would be willing to record a client testimonial. And yes, it's ok to incentivize them for their time.

Live Stream an Event

If you have an upcoming live event, fundraiser, speech, product demo, or convention—take a few minutes to record the event and upload it to your YouTube Channel.

Interviews and Team Profiles

One of the ways to connect and engage in our current digital world is to do an online interview or video profile. This can be short and sweet and answer a few questions. The goal is to make you and your team feel human and relatable. Also, take advantage of the opportunity to interview industry innovators you come across—and post the video to YouTube.

Mini-Commercials

Most small or mid-sized businesses do not have the budget to produce and place a TV commercial for local or nationwide placement, which makes YouTube videos the ideal alternative. In most cases, it is still best to have an online video expert produce and create your mini-commercial—including professional audio, voiceover, scripts, graphics, and editing. However, the price will be far more cost-effective than a commercial designed for TV. That being said, you can turn to DIY video tools to create white board videos, videos from images, or to edit the footage you shoot. Some of the best DIY video tools include:

- Nutshell
- Magisto
- Animoto
- Videoshop
- iMovie App
- iMovie for Macs

Videos That Support Your Content

As mentioned in the statistics in Chapter 1, when given the choice 59% of executives would rather watch a 30 to 120 second video—opposed to reading a blog post, article, or email. Also, email marketing campaigns with videos have a 96% higher email open rate. This means you should look for ways to create image, text, and white board videos that support your written content. The DIY tools above will help, or outsource to a video designer.

Share Your Story

Don't discount the value of sharing engaging content designed to share your company's story, or a story that will emotionally connect with your subscribers. For example, think of all the viral animal and baby videos that trend on YouTube. While babies and pets may not be relevant to your target audience, actively look for other ways to share stories that will brand your business in a positive light.

Mapping Out Your Video Content Plan

Use the video categories above to break your video content up in to relevant playlists, and map out how many videos you want to create each quarter. Your organic, and your paid, video marketing plan must be integrated with your entire online and social media marketing plan. For example, after your video goes live you can add it to an upcoming blog post— as well as sharing it to your other social media platforms.

Posting Videos Outside of YouTube

One of the unique things about video content, is that unlike blogs and articles—you can post the same video in multiple places online. Look for every opportunity to post your relevant videos, and remember that you can share them more than once. For example, if your "How To" video is a hit on Facebook—post it again in a week or two. This will help increase views, likes, comments and shares. Here are just a few places to post your videos:

- Facebook, Twitter, Instagram, Snapchat, LinkedIn, etc.
- Within articles and blog posts.
- Within relevant paid ads.
- Upload to relevant email marketing campaigns.
- Add to one-off relevant emails.
- Add to your newsletter.
- To relevant website pages.
- To the video section of your website.

Even if you have the option to add a video independently from the source file and not just from YouTube—upload the YouTube link. This will help to create more backlinks, and send more traffic back to your YouTube Channel.

Organically Optimizing Your YouTube Videos

Before you upload a new video to YouTube, you must make sure it is organically optimized. This is similar to optimizing your profile image and banner as detailed earlier, but a bit more in-depth.

Rename Your Video File

Before you upload your new video to YouTube, create an SEO optimized filename. Use Google Trends or a paid keyword tool to name and save your video with relevant keywords. For example, you may be tempted to name your videos chronologically—but "The Perfect Smokey Eye" is a better name than "Makeup Tutorial #12."

Input All Metadata

If you are familiar with filling out the metadata for your webpages and blog posts, it is somewhat similar within YouTube.

Title—your title needs to include the question and/or relevant keywords viewers will type in to YouTube when searching for the information your video provides. The more specific the better, just make sure your video name makes sense.

Description—Utilize the video description to highlight the key points within your video. While the description can be up to 5,000 characters—the first 160 characters (with spaces) is all that populates in search results. In other words, make sure there is a keyword or two in the first 160 characters. And don't forget to invite your viewers to subscribe to your Channel!

Captions and Subtitles—search engines can't crawl for videos, but they *can* crawl and index your captions and subtitles so make sure they are SEO optimized.

Tags and Categories—filling out the related tags and categories is just one more way to get your videos showing up organically in YouTube's search results and Up Next section.

Customize Your Video Thumbnail—add an optimized thumbnail to your videos as an often underutilized organic method of SEO.

Don't Forget to Add Links—be sure to add relevant external links to your video description. While you will certainly want to link back to your website, sales site, or other social media platforms—your organic performance will improve if you find quality links that are relevant to your video. For example, link back to the official source of your statistics.

Where many B2B and B2C marketers fail, is in uploading videos to YouTube *without* organically optimizing their files and metadata—and without a plan for posting their video content elsewhere. With the strategic approach above, and a steady stream of new videos, your subscription base and YouTube video views is sure to grow!

Now as great as all of this info is, it's not going to be of any use to you or your business if you don't apply what you've learned. So, roll up your sleeves and get ready to execute the steps in the following battle plan...

Battle Plan

Step 1: Spend an hour brainstorming your YouTube marketing goals.

Step 2: Think about what kind of videos are most useful for your business or niche and develop a content plan.

Step 3: Take 15 minutes to create and optimize a YouTube channel in accordance with what you learned in this guide.

Step 4: Start recording and uploading the first videos you decided on in step 2.

www.ingramcontent.com/pod-product-compliance
Lightning Source LLC
Chambersburg PA
CBRC090851210326
41597CB00011B/169